The Earth Avails

ALSO BY MARK WUNDERLICH

Voluntary Servitude
The Anchorage

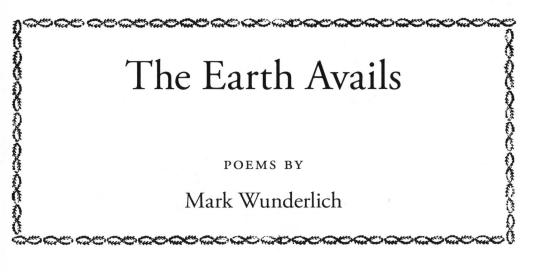

The Earth Avails

POEMS BY

Mark Wunderlich

Graywolf Press

This publication is made possible, in part, by the voters of Minnesota through a Minnesota State Arts Board Operating Support grant, thanks to a legislative appropriation from the arts and cultural heritage fund, and through grants from the National Endowment for the Arts and the Wells Fargo Foundation Minnesota. Significant support has also been provided by Target, the McKnight Foundation, Amazon.com, and other generous contributions from foundations, corporations, and individuals. To these organizations and individuals we offer our heartfelt thanks.

Published by Graywolf Press
250 Third Avenue North, Suite 600
Minneapolis, Minnesota 55401

www.graywolfpress.org

Published in the United States of America

ISBN 978-1-55597-666-8

2   4   6   8   9   7   5   3   1
First Graywolf Printing, 2014

Library of Congress Control Number: 2013946922

Cover design: Kyle G. Hunter

Cover art: Eggert Pétursson, Untitled, 2009. 170 x 170 cm, oil on canvas. Owned privately. Used with the permission of the artist.

For my parents

Contents

Once I Walked Out   3

Heaven-Letter   4

Coyote, with Mange   6

Waumandee   7

Dwell in My House   8

Stone Arabia   10

Driftless Elegy   12

A Servant's Prayer   17

Prayer for a Journey by Sea   20

Sand Shark   22

Cat Lying in the Grass   24

Prayer for Sunshine during a Time of Rain   25

Ram   28

Prayer in a Time of Drought   30

Palatine Bridge   32

Opening the Hive   34

Prayer for the Fruits of the Field   36

Raccoon in a Trap   38

Prayer during a Storm   39

Wild Boar   41

Heaven-Letter   43

The Corn Baby   45

A Husband's Prayer   46

Winter Study   48

Feral   50

Fire, Abate Thy Flames   51

Fire-Letter   52

Prayer for a Birthday   54

January Thaw   57

Lent   59

White Fur   62

Prayer in a Time of Sickness   63

Hwæt, eorðe mæg wið ealra wihta gehwilce
and wið andan and wið æminde
and wið þa micelan mannes tungan.

The earth avails against all creatures,
and against injury, and against forgetfulness,
and against the mighty tongue of man.

—*from the Anglo-Saxon Bee Charm*

The Earth Avails

Once I Walked Out

Once I walked out and the world
rushed to my side. The willows bent

their pliable necks, tossed green hair hugely.
The hawk cried by the well.

The crows kept counting their kind.
Once I walked out and the sheep

bleated with sensitivity, touched
black muzzles to the grass.

I was followed by dogs, by flies,
by horses both curious and spiteful.

The field of beans worked its sums
under green, the corn licked the air to haze.

I said good-bye to the house
with its sagging porch, attic hung with bats.

Good-bye braided rug, rabbit hutch, corn popper, copper tub.
The green world greened around me—

Virginia creeper, crown vetch, thistle, mullein, sumac.
I was full in my limbs, my laugh, pinkish skin.

I swung my arms, pulled air into lungs—
pine pollen, dust mote, mold spore, atomized dew—

bright wheel of flame twisting in the heavens
flushing the eye with light.

Heaven-Letter

You, looking down upon us from your canopy of air, to you
I commend my body and my brain, and that of my beloveds,

all that I own—stonepile of a house, tilting barn, garden and beloved beasts,
orchards, woods, my sweet furred animals,

the white mare and the brindled gelding,
the goats with their worldly eyes,

my reading and teaching from the books I read—
let it all rest in your giant hand.

You hang your lantern in the far window for me to see
until the cool blue of night burns and all the world is awake.

With your sorghum broom you sweetened my path, pulled
the woolen shawl around me while I slept.

That the lightning struck the willow
and did not fall—for this I am grateful.

Help me to work. When I mow or plant,
when I seal the summer fruits in jars,

slaughter or pluck, slit the rabbit's throat, butcher the fallow hen,
when I mend my rended garments, stitch the blanket top,

it is for you. When I wash or scrub upon my knees,
it is to see you more clearly. Each drop of sweat, each muscle pull is yours.

When I tilt my head to gossip,
sting my fleshy tongue.

Your unseen ones have linked willowy arms, drawn knives
tipped with stars and cut down the rat snake coiled in the cellar beams.

They have kept the unleashed Rottweiler from turning down our lane.
Bless Carlos, sharpening his saw in the yard, his night-lamp the emblem of
    your favor.

There is much for which I am ashamed.
Your invisible world surrounds me.

Let me aid the bachelor neighbors and the harelip with her stupid dog,
the tinker with his yard of noise, and the shape that parts the curtains

of the empty house across the marsh.
With your brush of feathers dust away my footprints.

Stay with me, here in the house.
Urge, with your holy claw, the scratching of my pen.

i don't like this one.

Coyote, with Mange

Oh, Unreadable One, why
have you done this to your dumb creature?
Why have you chosen to punish the coyote

rummaging for chicken bones in the dung heap,
shucked the fur from his tail
and fashioned it into a scabby cane?

Why have you denuded his face,
tufted it, so that when he turns he looks
like a slow child unhinging his face in a smile?

The coyote shambles, crow-hops, keeps his head low,
and without fur, his now visible pizzle
is a sad red protuberance,

his hind legs the backward image
of a bandy-legged grandfather, stripped.
Why have you unhoused this wretch

from his one aesthetic virtue,
taken from him that which kept him
from burning in the sun like a man?

Why have you pushed him from his world into mine,
stopped him there and turned his ear
toward my warning shout?

Waumandee

A man with binoculars
fixed a shape in the field
and we stopped and saw

the albino buck browsing
in the oats—white dash
on a page of green,

flick of a blade
cutting paint to canvas.
It dipped its head

and green effaced the white,
bled onto the absence that
the buck was—animal erasure.

Head up again, its sugar legs
pricked the turf, pink
antler prongs brushed at flies.

Here in a field was the imagined world
made visible—a mythical beast
filling its rumen with clover

until all at once it startled,
flagged its bright tail—
auf Wiedersehen, surrender—

and leapt away—
a white tooth
in the closing mouth of the woods.

Dwell in My House

Dwell in my house. Take up your spot in the tightest of corners,
in the crumbling cow-hair plaster mending the wall. Be found

bound in the blackest nook of the hearth from which
the intelligent eyes of the cats peer forth.

With your care, do dwell there, for otherwise I will be lost,
left to wander the brackish marsh of doubt

left to nurse my small resentments, arguing with no one
while I hoe the sow thistles from betwixt the rows of greens.

Come to me with your palms turned up, your brown hair
pulled back from that open face,

your ring of golden keys ready
to unlock the houses of the Patriarchs.

Snuff out the tomato blight, the beetles in the corn, call the wrens
with their needle beaks to eat the green worms

ciphering the cabbages' leaves.
Pour down on us the soft water of your rain.

Build your room inside me, for I do suffer.
When I am sleepless and tally what I have lost,

or when I feel for nodes swelling in my groin,
lay your hand upon my brow and shut the hot lids of my eyes.

When I hurry to lock my door, stay my hand.
When I see my aging, childless body,

bring me back to the company I keep.
All this will be taken from me, this I know.

There is more for me to suffer, though I wait for you to bare yourself,
to touch that bloody muscle in your chest.

Stone Arabia

The horses bisect the field
pull the cutting plow,
        guided burden, churning
                a soil-fold, wave of earth
                    turned up

        for the gulls to pick; they
follow the farmer, cut the
        April air with hollow-boned wings
                scurrying beetles,
                        grubs and red worms
                            the wages

        for following the plow's wake.
The field turns from tan and
        green-flecked
                to uniform brown,
                        lowliest color on the wheel

        offset by a fencerow
where the wren's syrinx bursts
        with the air-blast
                of a tiny lung—wind thimble
                        muscle-trill—warbling with
                            the sexual urge to build.

Black cows punctuate
the green page of pasture,
    move in cued diagrams,
        knee-deep in spring-flush,
            mouths bent to grass, growing
                the soft bones of fetal calves
                    on alfalfa, white clover

which they pull
from the fallow field
    while the whiff
        of their sweet-smelling shit
            is wound in the spool
                of this sentence.

Driftless Elegy

The bridge over the Mississippi is shut,
the traffic diverted to Wabasha

while authorities investigate the undergirding
which is corroded and in danger of collapse.

Work has slowed on both sides of the river
while an enterprising man with a pontoon boat

ferries people from side to side. Fountain City
has long been without a grocery store; Abt's Market

closed when I was a child. The owner whistled,
and the women who worked the front counter

tracked everyone's movements through the town,
gazing out the plate glass windows with awnings

shielding them from the sun. In Minneapolis
the coast guard climbs into a Suburban

and makes the trip to Winona to arrest the man
with the boat. What he's doing is illegal, he's told.

"You try to help folks out and all you get is a kick in the ass."
The grocery is gone, the brewery is gone, gone

the house where my father was born,
gone the warehouse where we hung deer in November,

gone the shop with its cigar boxes full of bolts,
hinges, flanges, copper wire, ball bearings, or anything

someone might have saved for projects yet to be imagined.
The cellar where the washtubs bubbled to keep

the baitfish alive—one full of bullheads, one of minnows,
where geraniums overwintered, where the dug bulbs

of tulips were gnawed by muskrats during floods—
that has been filled and paved. A gas pump stands

where the glider rocked, a lit sign where the bridle wreath
once cast its white profusion to the sun.

❧

The sheep are gone from Grandma Haney's pasture.
The last badger was shot from Wiggy Stuber's field.

There's no money in milk anymore, and you marry your herd
anyhow, and who wants to be that bound to anything

that won't love you back? The Gold'n Plump plant expands
in Arcadia, and the owners go to Mexico to recruit.

You know the workers by the angry rash
from fingertip to shoulder, enflamed by chicken water

seeping inside their arm-length plastic gloves.
The bluffs are covered in cedars since no one grazes

anything there anymore.

❧

Who will remember the lodge hall and the good times had there?
Who will remember the handshake for the Rebeccas?

No one visited the museum, so the society put it up for sale.
A millionaire hangs cottages from the bluffs,

rents them to businessmen who drive here from Chicago or Milwaukee
to hunt the deer that breed and fatten at the edges of fallow fields.

The heads are left with the taxidermist, the meat dropped off at the church.
Old houses go vacant, new ones get built—ugly, vaulted ceilings,

windows the full two stories of their angular fronts
that jut like glass barge prows from the bluffs.

❧

Hilbert is dead. Mutz is dead. Chester has turned to crumbs in his grave.
No one remembers when Babe Schwark died

and Bootie Schmidt is up to the Home for good.
Piggy is long gone, Home his headstone says.

The inveterate drinkers warm barstools at the Golden Frog,
and only those from "away" have anything to do with the Monarch.

Mother's sweater sat unsold in the gift shop
until Papa reclaimed it in a huff.

The property dispute over the mule pasture fence
has finally run its course; no one wins

though the surveyor got struck by lightning and is dead.
The old steamboat dry-docked in Winona

got hauled to the landfill, and someone trained lights
on the outcropping of Sugar Loaf bluff to form, at night,

the jagged outline of a cross.

There are those who claim the DNR
has let loose breeding pairs of mountain lions

in the bluffs around Waumandee. The warden says
that's nonsense, but why would anyone believe him?

Someone burned down the Chicken Valley strip club,
where the girl who won the state cross-country meet

ended up pole dancing, and where her drivers ed teacher
and basketball coach went to watch her on Friday nights.

The Road Dogs host a car shoot to raise money
for a cancerous friend: put a car in neutral,

roll it down a hill, and for $10 you get to shoot the car
as many times as you can. Helps if you're drunk.

A well-meaning ornithologist opened a raptor center
as a local attraction, populated it with the dumb and clumsy,

unlucky birds electrocuted by power lines, shot by moral derelicts
with crossbows, the poisoned, those whose taste for road kill

tangled them with a car. The eagles hop awkwardly around their pens,
glare through the wire, their talons like pruning shears

gripping the perches of what will be
their last home.

I am the end of a genetic line—a family dies with me.
This is hardly a tragedy. We are not an impressive group,

in intellect or physical form. With weak hearts, myopic,
we paddle lazily down the human genome,

pausing to root briefly here on the riverbank
in the shade of these limestone bluffs.

In an early photograph I have, part of the town
goes up in flames—a premonition from the 1880s.

A group of women, corseted, skirts infested with lace,
watch from behind a buckboard as ash flings itself

into the sky. To the right the blur of a girl
rushes away like a ghost. No face. Hardly a form.

Just a hat and a dress, and the news of a fire,
though no one is alive who knows her name.

A Servant's Prayer

Oh Tenderhearted, O Kindhearted,
you who have spared us from eternal servitude,

by torturing and killing your only child—
we know what you can do.

Only you can spare us
from a world in which the Creature

presses his stinking hoof to our neck,
the tyrant who supervises a petty bureaucracy

rich with oil and other filth, covers his sow-bride's
fat Bahamas-tanned paw with a crust of diamonds.

You have chosen to keep me in a state
of service, beholden to a mustachioed czarina

isolated and confused and grandiose,
which is, I confess, a trial.

I beg you, assuage my bitterness.
Help me to know that this is your will,

and keep me from resenting
those, who despite their meager talents,

their pettiness and appetite for derision,
wield power over me. My service here,

though of this world, is not meant for this world
bent of uglification and strife.

Part the curtain and let me glimpse
your gleaming hem.

Remind me that behind this knotted tapestry
of tasks and humiliations

is a shining world that must remain hidden
so it may remain unspoiled. When Misti

severed her thumb and wrapped it
is a swaddle of cloth, afraid to tell management

lest she lose her job, I glimpsed you,
there at the pearly bone flush with crimson,

beautiful and fragile and lit with the pain
of our kind. At the hospital, she was made whole

again, though I'm certain she bears the scar to this day.
You were secreted, once again,

beneath the surgeon's arrogant work.
I am grateful for the power in my body;

help guard it from poisons, keep my sleeve
far from the spinning shaft, my skin free from

tick bites, stray dogs, the mule's twisting
ivory teeth. Help me keep my strength,

and practice diligence and mercy,
like your son, sawing and swinging his hammer,

walking home on dusty feet
to a meal someone worked all morning

to prepare.

Prayer for a Journey by Sea

Look at me from your pitiless distance, look
as I give myself to the feral sea

where I hang between atmosphere
and the hidden sands below, your fool in this

plaything of a boat, which may no longer save nor salvage.
See me here, face in my hands

wet with spray and sweat, sick with the knowledge
of my unworthiness. The wind pitches,

waves break where they will, neither soil nor stone
beneath me, while overhead the dumb sky strips off

its wet shirt and tosses it to the wind's hands.
I beg you, push up my chin with your thumb

and press your bearded cheek to mine. Settle me
with the dark soil of your eyes, you who made us

and all the other pieces of the damaged world.
What we men offer each other is nothing

compared to your cold body lying down atop my own,
prostrate on the deck, your breath humid in my ear.

Last night I dreamt the ship grew down and pinions,
a hard and rubbery bill, while the prow shook itself

into the neck of a swan. I clung to its back like a louse
and we flew, feet drawn up into feathers,

the glacier of night creeping by beneath us.
I have forsworn all the others, feel you

tightening me to your large thighs,
nothing left to keep us apart.

I am your little ram,
burying his muzzle in thick grass of your pasture,

folded by you at night, herded by day,
a dedicated dog nipping at my hocks.

The day will come for you to draw
the bright sickle of the moon

across my wooly throat.
Do it with love, without regret.

Sand Shark

It rose up
nosing from the bottom
of the bay
hook in its mouth,
slothful, circling
in a whirl
through murk,
salt, krill.
It pulled at the line
but did not fight—
no fit as I turned the reel.
Long as my arm
it countered clockwise
as I drew it—
slick thought
up from the dark
reach of green
and mollusk bed,
up from where it fed
on what dropped
down, what fell
to the wavering floor.
In my shock
I wondered whether
to cut the line,
or to pry hook and lure
from its throat,
from between the needled
snags of its mouth
designed to hold

all that entered
and ferry it to the red
chambers of its gut.
I cut
the line, nudged
the sluggish creature
with my foot
and slipped it
back into the bay,
its appetite torn
by the barb of my hook.
My hands were slicked
with blood and slime
and though I washed
its briny tang
clung to me
for a time.

Cat Lying in the Grass

He would lie in the grass
    belly-down, needled paws
        poised to take his prey, which
            more often than not
was large—grouse or rabbit kit,
    blue jay, mole, vole or bat.
        He left the snakes alone
            to dream in the hay mow,
                eyes dusty with sun.
The dogs would, if young and stupid,
    follow him in the yard,
        keeping a distance until,
            reluctantly it seemed,
                he'd burst from a crouch
                    to shred their soft ears.
We shared territory in a state of truce—
    three pastures, two yards
        barn, shed and stable, the sheep pens,
            outer edges of the sty, marsh
              and forest and house,
                in which he'd sleep away
                    the powdery daylight.
Once, he split the nose
    of a curious woman
        who foolishly turned
            to see what wildness tore
               at the back of her chair.
                He was impossible to punish.

Prayer for Sunshine during a Time of Rain

You, the author of all truths, you
unbuttoning your coat of darkness,

why have you tied us in your sack
fashioned from the sheet of the sky?

We recall how your once washed the world
of its travails, in your fury, balling

your fist into your palm, you made the skies
crack and crumple into rain, leaving

only the mildest and most irascible creatures
who could fly or swim for days.

We know the harshness of your corrections.
We promise we will set to work

laundering the accumulated stains,
our hands red and puckered, pinning

up our inner garments to billow and snap
on the line, scrub the mold

etching its fresco on the plastered walls.
You have been kind, watching

us as we slept, our breath the ball you wind
on your giant hands. You, the Tenderest,

you who made the deep wells run cool,
then showed us heaven's countenance

reflected in the tin pail we drew up
from the depths, there in the springhouse,

where we chilled the milk hot
from the bodies of our beasts.

Take from us all of our misdeeds,
the shaming rain and mire.

The fields have eroded and the sky
exhausts herself day and night with crying.

The corn, stunted in the fields
presses green tongues to the sky,

desperate for a lick of sun, the garden bloats
and goes to seed, pebbled with slugs.

We know you are incapable of lying,
we remind you to keep to us your promise.

Don't withhold your affection, turn away
your face and let your rage

whiten the cords of your enormous neck.
Don't leave us with this meager meal, with nothing

sweet or fat to scrape across our bread.
We promise to be your good children,

your obedient children, and know
your anger is the other side of love,

for which we thank and praise you
all the days of our lives.

Ram

He stands stamping in the pasture,
angry that I've come, angry
that I didn't come sooner with my pail
of grain. A topnotch of wool shields his eyes,
snagged with bits of hay, bunched with burrs.
He shakes his head, flares nostrils under a Roman nose,
curls a lip to show me his single row
of teeth like keys of a harpsichord—long,
ivory-yellow, pegged in a black gum.
In snow, he'll stand all day
by the hay feeder, fleece parting at the spine,
grease saving him from the worst of it,
staring into the source of the weather.
In April the shearing team will come
and tip him on his rump, ridding him
of year's worth of wool. He'll submit
to the indignity,
his fleece peeled back in flocculent rolls.
Back on all fours, he'll trot off
to find his flock, sniff his harem's
bare behinds, account for his many lambs,
that nurse desperately, confused
by their mothers' altered forms.
They call and call, while he remains calm,
stepping among his kind
assessing the newly naked.
Once he knocked me down
with a blow to my hip, three hundred pounds
and a thick skull crashed against my pelvis.
Sprawled in the mud and dung

I pulled myself through straw
while he backed up for another run.
Before he could I hit him
with a broken rail, cracked it
across his nose. He barely noticed.
Now he regards me
with golden ovine eyes,
rich with a pastoral flame.

Prayer in a Time of Drought

You who has planted language on our tongues,
given us words then taught us how to beg;

this text is not mine alone, but one we have knotted together,
retted and broke and spun

and which we hope will find its way through the unknowable clouds
hoping to be opened and spread upon your lap,

the warp and weft admired and put to use.
I am your poor child, sickened by the heat,

unable to work or attend to my duties, the light
drawing my strength the way an onion draws a fever from a foot.

This morning, the air is still once again,
the sun dawns, shell pink, in a cloudless sky,

and I awake poorly rested, to look upon the garden
withering at the root, the lilies now a thatch of straw,

the bees scouring the inside of the pump for a drop of condensation,
while the hens pant and hold their wings akimbo

after pecking the limp green meal I offer them
in lieu of warming seeds or corn. It is hard not to see this as scorn,

your burning sentence written in the dying grass.
We understand your anger, though even innocents suffer,

the birds and beasts too dumb to understand
your finer points as they eat and rest and groom,

30

searching for a pool of shade in which
to suffer out the afternoon. It is not yet too late

to save the summer crops, stunted though they are
by what you withhold. We beg for the cooling sheet

to be lain upon our valley bed. Somewhere on your golden ring
is a key to unlock the shut door

that keeps the skies from opening
and cooling and sending the quenching,

sweet smelling rain, Father please.

Palatine Bridge

At Palatine Bridge the cemetery
is a field of broken teeth,

the names on the stones
long erased by the wind's hand.

As I walk the green square
locusts spring from my steps,

barely able to pull themselves
from their truculent chewing and breeding.

Semis downshift with a grunt,
whip the hollyhocks fronting the church.

No one's been put there for a hundred years.
It's a field of loss with a thick skin of turf.

Not half a mile away
a black Percheron mare lies in the ditch,

her harness still on,
wagon on its side, the knacker

called on a cell phone.
There's some blood from her velvet nose

but no mess, the beast's
muscular pull, her clever tender ears

undone at the blind curve—
animus pulled out—

a thorn bit
from the warm paw of morning.

Opening the Hive

Suited and veiled to see the queen
I bruise the air with smoke,
puff from a billow

the punkwood and cow horn sumac
I burn to stun the city
of sunlight that is the hive.

I am married to them—to it—
for they are one thing—
body in the shape of a box,

body in bits flung to the sky
or sipping water and nectar
with the tensile proboscis

used to clean and suck, that once
groomed the queen when she
was still foreign and caged

in her box of wire and candy.
She was womb without a body,
heart without a head, and now

she is their castle keep
calling her progeny
who scour the world for flowers.

They have built their comb
and attend their young,
have stored away in clammy cells—

antiseptic, condensed—
essence of shepherd's purse and grape.
They cluster round their monarch

lighting they air with prudence
and with rage.
A visitor was recently stung.

She stood too close, blocked a worker's path
and a bee collided with her head,
struck her on the arch of her brow.

I flicked away the stinger,
licked a penny and held it to the spot.
The hurt of it moved around her face

and the eye swelled shut
from the barb of life
torn from the body

of the bee.

Prayer for the Fruits of the Field

Show your leniency to the lovely fruits of the field.
Purify the air, send your soft rain and kindly weather

so that the crops may thrive. Keep from them
the poisonous blight, so that we and our animals

may eat. Curse the rat fouling the corn, the canker
that curls leaves, burn away the beetles that stripped

the cherry leaving a bouquet of twigs. Douse the mites
that choke the tracheas of the bees, the raccoon

with his taste for eggs, the fly-bitten buck
stripping the apple trees, the voles that stole the row

of beets stored under straw and ice.
Keep away the fevers and pests, poisons,

the ghost whose face of smoke yawns
from the cement factory stack,

Blow away the filth of men drifting through the valley
that threatens to embitter the berries, taint the wine

and spoil the grain, the humid wind
with its cargo of blighting spores. Through our own avarice

and bad luck, we eat misfortune dusted
over meals served up on white china plates.

Protect us from the plagues of the spirit,
help us to rise for work, set the cap on our heads,

and face the list of tasks with diligence and good cheer.
Keep the wars on opposite shores,

spare us from wandering, hungry soldiers
cut loose from all that keeps a man

from doing his worst. Help us to keep our promises,
and remain hopeful, and let us see

the abundant fruits as the fountain
and increase of the green shoots

of kindness awakened from dormant kernels
in our heads.

Raccoon in a Trap

The kidskin of his clever paws,
charcoal black and clawed like a witch,

scratch at the turf. Hanging his head
he hunches like a bear and in his fur turns

a boggy funk, a whiff like the hairy belly
of a man. I carry the cage to the edge of the woods

and he barks, bares a grin of sharps,
points a flinty nose, moist and smart

to read his future on the air. I believe
this is the thief who stole the nest of chicks,

tore the vent from a hen and ate her
in the company of her peers—a husbandman's

springtime menace, the glowing eyes
in the night. In the orchard, morning clouds

disperse. The sun returns for another run
pulled by the beasts of myth

before I put the muzzle of the gun through the wires
and fill his warm head with lead.

Prayer during a Storm

You, the strongest, you swimming in the clouds
and churning in the soil,

this storm with its electricity and crashing thunder
reminds us of your fury and disappointment.

You call us through wind and thunder, from which
all creatures tremble and hide themselves in their dens

or in cellars, the birds clinging to branches,
or huddling under the eaves of our vulnerable roofs,

the cats tearing into the mattress ticking from below.
We hear you, angry at your forge, your hammer

crashing and the bellows making the sparks fly.
We reach for our sorry ways like a willful child

reaching for a firebrand, surprised to be burnt,
astonished to feel the heat for days.

We see what you did when you dropped your
funnel onto the hillside cemetery and tossed

the headstones like a handful of broken teeth, uprooted the yew trees
like a gardener pulling nettles from a ditch,

choosing to spare us, while exhibiting your scorn
with what's left of the dead. We lift up our faces, beg

for you to look upon us and spare our imperfect bodies,
our houses, yards and gardens, our town

with its proclivity for floods and mosquitoes,
its counterpane of fog, and its cooling view

of the Donderberg crossed by a rusty train.
Spare the orchards from hail, the pines

from lightning, the village from the river's brush
painting the cellars with mud. Spare us too

from a painful death, and keep us
from doing our worst by ciphering your word

in the sky with your stylus of light,
the atmosphere reciting in a booming choir.

Wild Boar

Meat. Bristled hide that can't be called skin,
never skin—too bristled for that, too dry.
Hooves dainty as a doe's. Furred ears.
Rusty wool along the belly. Their shape
sharp and narrow, an axe of muscle,
bottled urge. Two tusks sickle up
from the split of a whiskery maw.
Here at the game farm, they mill and snuffle,
tear the corn shuck bale to bits. Pigeons
and sparrows make the atmosphere overhead,
chipping at the air, cobwebbed beams.
These beasts do not doze the way a pork chop
hog will doze, like a meat pie on a concrete plate.
Here, piglets daubed with racing stripes
clamp their nozzles to a tit
sucking with sleepless vigor
while the boar eases out a penis big as my wrist.
Acorn snout, mallow root snout,
salsify snout, snout tuned to road kill
or wobbly fawn or grouse chicks
peppering the leaf-mold. Snout subtle
and kaleidoscopic sniffing the array of green,
of decay, of seed or breeding. Three seasons ago
a sow escaped. Heavy with pigs, she bedded down
by the creek in a blizzard. Twenty below,
she set to work and tore up grass and brush
to make a nest big as an igloo, in which
she lay down to farrow seven pigs
deep in the warm center of her den.
They remained safe until the farmer found them out
and brought them wriggling in a sack to the barn.

The sow followed, her need to mother
trumping the will to root and wallow,
trot her litter across a stubbled field
the trail of a promise in her nose.

Heaven-Letter

For years the letter was lost somewhere inside the city walls. We the citizens scoured the towers, cellars, narrow alleys where thieves lurked, rats nosed the dark with shell-pink snouts. It was nowhere to be found. It was, as has been said, written in letters of gold on the air and would hang like a cobweb of glass above the font in the Magdalene's church. If you wished to copy it, the unseen ones would dip their quills in the lake of fire, and begin to write.

I will tell you what it said, though I trembleth at the task.

First, look for my hand of Nothing moving in the darkness. When you are alone, it reaches toward you.

Next, I do not wish to see you comb the snarls from Vanity's wig. The names of the poorest are tattooed on my breast; give freely to them.

Praise be to Melchior! There are six days of the week for you to finish your work, sweep the chaff from the granary floor, turn the bedposts on the lathe, poison the vixen in her den, six to shear or card or spin. On the seventh, I want you on your knees, my unimaginable face the white sheet of thought, single cloud, ice vapor, pushing through the firmament.

There are places where my name is no longer recorded—Katusha, Kalashnikov—forked tongues of steel and ash. Weevils spoil the unshipped grain, moss grows in the plaster of the flooded house.

Take yourself early to the holy places.

All that you acquire can easily burn. The usurers, the oil magnates, war profiteers, rapists, plunderers of my garden—their names are well-known to me.

For those who take pleasure in the suffering of others—cigarette burn, snarling dog, pulling tight the cord of the hood—your profane smiles will be broken.

This is written in my own hand.

I look through you and see your troubles, thick in the saw grass, wriggling in the shallow pool of thought.

One day I will ask you my burning question, and your answer must be ready, jewel on the tongue.

Keep this letter within the four walls of your house. I can extinguish fires, stay the muddy water of a flood. When on your person, weapons cannot harm you.

The Corn Baby

They brought it. It was brought
from the field, the last sheaf, the last bundle

the latest and most final armful. Up up
over the head, hold it, hold it high, it held

the gazer's gaze, it held hope, did hold it.
Through the stubble of September, on shoulders

aloft, hardly anything, it weighed, like a sparrow,
it was said, something winged, hollow, though

pulsing, freed from the field
where it flailed in wind, where it waited, wanted

to be found and bound with cord. It had
limbs, it had legs. And hands. It had fingers.

Fingers and a face peering from the stalks,
shuttered in the grain, closed, though just a kernel,

a shut corm. They brought him and autumn
rushed in, tossed its cape of starlings,

tattered the frost-spackled field.

A Husband's Prayer

You, author of all wonders,
shown to us by your many prophets

and instruments—our own shoemaker's daughter,
illiterate and bent, who proclaims from her special chair

in the meetinghouse, who reminds us to be humble,
and not aspire above our station,

to find beauty in utility, and to beware idolatry—
you who chose to provide me with a spouse,

and a house, a barn and sheds, gardens,
a small orchard, a field rich with clover,

hives humid and speckled with pollen,
and who finds the greatest satisfaction

when we attend to three responsibilities:
to be a brother to another, to be a good

and kindly neighbor, to move through the world
with a mate; give me strength.

From the coolest and boggiest portion
of my heart, my worries multiply as spores

canker the apple leaf. My mate,
though weak, is there to help me

set aside my burdens, if only I could
describe them into the space between our pillows

at night. When thistles spring up in the field
or our marriage, when the noxious vine

twines onto the maple, let us pull it up
by it roots. When I gaze upon the gothic script

tattooed on the young gardener's brown stomach,
strain to read it as it folds, remind me

my own name is written in the mind of another
however faint.

Let that be enough. Let me not dwell
on our weaknesses, on our smells, our shedding

skin and hair. There is a small chalet
somewhere on the cool green pasture

of an alp where we shelter, our heads
on the striped ticking, our hands

barely touching as we sleep.

Winter Study

Two days of snow, then ice
and the deer peer from the ragged curtain of trees.

Hunger wills them, hunger
pulls them to the compass of light

spilling from the farmyard pole.
They dip their heads, hold

forked hooves
above snow, turn furred ears

to scoop from the wind
the sounds of hounds, or men.

They lap at a sprinkling of grain,
pull timid mouthfuls from a stray bale.

The smallest is lame, with a leg
healed at angles, and a fused knob

where a joint once bent.
It picks, stiff, skidding its sickening limb

across the ice's dark platter.
Their fear is thick as they break a trail

to the center of their predator's range.
To know the winter

is to ginger forth from a bed in the pines,
to search for a scant meal

gleaned from the carelessness
of a killer.

Feral

She arrived one night
to sit on the step

before the dawn chased her
and she went to crouch

in the dark barn. Little heart-shaped
face, fulled and furred,

peers from the box we made
for her. Rheumy-eyed,

tattered ear, she tips
to hear a bird chipping

in the ribs of the stripped brush,
pushed back into her bed of straw.

Now she's gone off
into undergrowth

and a coyote left his tracks
as a mark.

Where she's off to, or how she'll fare
I cannot know or say.

Fire, Abate Thy Flames

We watched the conflagration from the hill.

When the wind turned, ash rained into our hair.

The building's keepers rushed to quell the flames;

we did nothing, settling in for the show.

Once solid, the warehouse became a cloud

reflecting its unmaking.

It huffed and groaned like a bear as it changed its shape

until the fire took the building in its arms

and it rose.

Fire-Letter

The following is the invention of one Egyptian, picked up in a security sweep of a hotel in Cairo, sold by independent contractors to the occupying authorities. Transported to an unspecified location in a republic formerly part of the Soviet Union, he, along with six of his countrymen, were sentenced to hang. The seventh of them was a man of eighty years, condemned to be beheaded on the sixteenth of the month.

A conflagration created from the mishandling of a generator caused a great fire to break out at the former Soviet military base. This turned out to be the seventh's good luck! The old man was liberated, taken to the fire for the purpose of having him try his arts and mysterious workings.

What he accomplished astonished all present. Within a quarter of an hour, by holy miracle, he stayed the conflagration. For this, he was pardoned, taken by night transport to Syria where he disappeared. His whereabouts are unknown, though given his age, the difficulty of travel in an unstable region, many assume him to be dead.

His words have been recorded here. I offer them to you now.

> You, burning one, Heart of the Desert, conflagration and appetite, sun fragment—welcome, you fiery guest, do not grasp further, but spare the rest.

> Guest, I count this fire to your ransom. All the invisible ones are here behind me. Can you hear the rattling of their silver pinions? The hush of them?

> I command you, by the power of the great Perfectionist, the one who does all this well, the plumb builder, the one who knows but speaks not, the maker of all you see, all that is inside and outside your ken: Stand still, Proceed no further. A man once stood in a river and was washed and washed until he was clean; that I count to your ransom, O Tongue of Heat, purveyor of Ash.

Somewhere in a dark interior courtyard, amid the plashing of a fountain, having put her children down for the afternoon, a young mother turns her attention to the tending of the garden: Lush tendrils, succulents, rare and old varietals, flowers of a subtle shape and fragrance, a neat potager in quadrants with a pear tree blooming in the center, a dovecote purring and chucking in the noon heat. Think of her. In her name, I tell you, cease your rage. Now, that the courtyard and mother are fixed in your terrible and hollowing mind, I count this as part of your ransom.

Set aside your violence—let it drop like gloves onto a hall table. So much blood has been spilt, so much of it sweet and dear. In our names it has trickled through streets, been washed into the gutters with broken glass and dung long after the wounded have been loaded into the screaming white trucks, the dead covered until their relatives could be found. And for what? I tell you, in their name I command you, stop.

Once I stared at you in wonder. Now, you are the figure in the center of the folded petals of the night-blooming cereus—hidden, in perpetual repose. You, and those who made you, pull us from this lake of fire. Keep this land with its orchards and vines in a state of happy work. Keep the wasting disease from us, the bog-spavins and the croup. All that bites and stings and slithers—be gone.

Whoever keeps this letter in his house will not suffer from conflagrations. Pregnant women who keep this letter on their person will not be susceptible to charmers, sorcerers, the ill-willed and invisible, delusions. Keep this letter and you will be untouched by disease. In his name, I swear this is true.

Prayer for a Birthday

My privilege and my proof, pressing your eternal skin to mine—
I feel your fingers touching down on the crown of my head

where I pray they remain during this life and in the next.
The intricacies of your world astound me.

You flickered through the rooms where my mother dwelt,
when I was naked and formless as a seal, sensitive

to the tides of her body. I did not come too early onto land,
did not emerge until my days were written

on the translucent pages of your enormous book.
The great lid of your eye peeled back to see I was not yet whole.

I remember today the day of my birth.
Your words washed that which clung to me from the other side,

bound to me the promised ghost.
I was dipped and sponged, cut free,

delivered as I was like a lamb lodged in his dam. Tears and pain
were her price, and I was handed over to be wiped with straw.

You built me, bone by bone, counting
the hairs that would one day thatch my crown,

building cleverness in my hands, weakness in my knees,
a squint and a taste for cake. You showed me

the dip of a man's clavicle, arrow of ankle and calf,
weaving in me a love of those bodies like my own,

yet not mine. When you turned to your next task
a shadow crossed the room stirred from the muddy banks

rimed with ice. In the spot where my skull was soft
it set down its stylus and inked a bruise—

a scrap used to blot a leaking pen. Since then
my mind has raced toward the brink, spun

and knit and torn out the same silvery threads
only to wind them up again. Still, the bargain

you made without my consent has left me
here to ponder your airy limbs striding through the sky,

the red rustle of your gown. A season ago, I looked out upon the verdure
of the small meadow below the house—boggy in parts—

the pollard willows gnarling and sipping from gnat-speckled pools,
the turkeys scratching under the sweep of green

as it prepared to die back for another year, littered with mute papery tongues.
You are easier to see when you denude your world with decay.

And so I saw you there, flashed in the shallow water,
parting the curtain of the willow fronds and warming my face with light.

My mother and father call me and sing,
sweet and tuneless, their voices worn down by your turning wheel.

You have kept us together for half a man's natural years,
these last the tenderest as their bodies

break and their minds dip deeper into dust
to bring forth the features of distance.

My day will be spent here, in the middle of things,
feeding split logs into the stove, cats coiling through rooms

as the snow ticks at the windows' double panes.
I will read a book with snow at its center,

in a forest lost inside a forest in the north, the sun
an afterthought in the darkest days of the year.

I am thankful for all that buffers me from the cold,
all that binds me to my clan,

though I see a future strange and tuneless
as I push forward into the mind's blinding field of white.

January Thaw

The bees flare up
on a warm January day,
take short flight,

streak the snow
with rusty excrement.
Once the ice is cleared

from the door of the hive
they begin to move their dead,
push their crumpled bodies out the door.

They form a little mound,
rounded forms a payment
to the sun climbing low

though promising a future.
I hold my ear to the box
expecting to hear a hum

but the bees are dumb in their closet
of wood and wax.
Inside they tend a world of sun

and flowers, botanical sex
stored, condensed, excreted.
They nurse their cells, sweetened

in the month of May,
tear off caps to dip a proboscis in
what they alone can make—

antiseptic, immune to rot.
Somewhere in the center
which I cannot see, they ball up

around their fertile queen. She rests
and waits, licked and petted
by her many daughters,

her mate's penis absorbed
into her thorax
after she tore it from him

as she was meant to do—
prize or payment—
a mile up in the sky.

Lent

I saw the jaundiced fist of rhubarb
punch through the February crust

there in the corner bed where I spread
the wood ashes. Its crenellations

tendered through mud and grit.
A bit of leaf-mold crowned it.

The cardinal sweet-sang
to the elongated day

from behind his night-black mask.
The woods graying still,

a forest of beams. Cold tamps sap
back down the taproot.

The titmouse pips a seed hull.
The cherry swells a node

of red and the hive stokes
the chip of sun that is their queen.

Three months back the world
was undone, flesh starved

to sinew. We spent our days
swaddled in wool and down,

banking the plate-stove with cedar
to remake summer's heat

on our outstretched hands.
The night sent up a tallow disk

and constellations bridged
the unknowable. We chose our meals

from among the globes of fruit
sweetened under glass in the pantry.

Look now as the world swims back.
Down the road reddish lambs

butt heads, nurse the swelled bag
of their dam. By the road, the remains

of a fox appear as the gray
snow peels back, recoiling

from the sun.
A bit of wind

noses the fur, as I pick
the skull to prop atop the stone wall.

Does the vixen sleep
alone in her den? Will she whelp

another litter of kits,
or will she keep her face

tucked in the stole of her tail
and rot away the summer

soundless but for
the blowfly's repetition

as it transports her portion bit by bit
into the warming sky?

White Fur

In the town of my childhood, little of note ever happened
so when the albino deer was found drowned in the slough

having been driven onto the punky ice by dogs,
the game warden brought the dead beast to the school.

I might have been seven or maybe six years old.
I suppose we were made to line up—

since that is how we were moved from place to place—
and were directed out the industrial doors

to admire the animal sprawled in the back of a truck.
We gathered around it, its whiteness a world

bled of distinction, its eyes pink and drying
in the prairie air. We were told we could touch it

and these many years since that March day, I can still
see my hand, pink and small, buried into the white fur

of the buck's neck, crackling with static
and coming to life with the electric surge

that animates all things. Later, the buck
would be mounted and placed in a glass case in the bank,

which is where the town kept things that were precious.
Behind it, the art teacher rendered the bluffs in oils

with the fussy hand of a miniaturist, and the buck
remains there today, in perpetual imitation of itself.

Prayer in a Time of Sickness

So far I have warded off the worst of things
that can happen to a brain and to a body.

I have loved my self and the world more than I have loved you,
with your unknowable face in the firmament,

and the world ripe with detail.
What is it you wish to teach me?

My life has been one of tasks, listed
and attended, materials curried and weeded and laid by.

I have been diligent and have done my work.
Then, a day came when I could not answer

the letter of a friend, could not offer my help,
read to the end of the sentence. The phoebe

tossed from his nest was broken on vulpine teeth,
spirited into the undergrowth in the dark,

then the six fat wrens in their house hung in the arbor
disappeared and their parents stopped their singing.

Weeds grew, and I ignored my chores,
while the cat worried her tail of its most plumescent fur.

I saw my body, white as tallow,
my face framed by colorless hair,

noted my appetites, then put them aside,
walked and walked to wear it all away.

In the bin, last year's potatoes grew their eyes
without benefit of soil or sun,

and I spent another night awake and unrested,
knitting a cap for a child come too early

into the world. What lies on the other side?
What do I need to know that will keep me anchored,

admired as I am from a distance—
an image false as a tin star?

I yearned to be cast up on an arctic island, bare of trees,
populated by the recalcitrant

and their flocculent, half-wild beasts,
the air dry and howling, cliffs exposed, the wind

stirring its cauldron of birds. You have written
each of my days into your illumined book,

though I believe this portion will remain unread,
a page torn out and stuffed into a crack

to keep out the winter damp.
I was built by the love of my mother,

then let go. She is now old and sleeps much of the day
like a cat, eats small meals in her chair,

bakes for funerals or dusts the small museum
visited only by accident.

And so she serves the ghosts of our town
and does not believe in you at all.

❧

At summer's end, I traveled north,
crossed the sea, to the salted rim of the Arctic.

From a rented room, I watched revelers wend in arcs
bound by the corrugated street,

breakfasted on liver paste and beets,
rode tinted in the light of a city bus

as it ferried me to the national attractions:
a heroic past reconstructed in wax,

diorama of a seeress wearing cat-skin gloves
dining on the hearts of dogs,

spidery manuscripts chilled under glass,
and the rusted nails and altarpieces

standing in for an architecture
long effaced by the wind's hand.

❧

A young man named for a god of fucking
rode his palomino next to my dun.

His face was chapped and his hair
was combed by the wind from underneath

a helmet of foam. We passed the named steadings
roofed in turf, the pyramids of hay

while our horses muscled like athletes
on paths cut through knee-high grass,

over lava and hill crest, past geyser
and sulphurous marsh, horned sheep

wandering wild through wind and rain.
Hours went by and no one spoke

as our animals huffed and pushed
against the reins. My thighs tightened

on my gelding's furred back, hands
learned his mouth like that of a husband.

Your hold on this island is tenuous,
broken as it is by the core of the earth

seeping its sulphurous reek and sanding the air with ash.
The inhabitants live amongst the greatest powers

visible to their water and ice colored eyes.
You, our Maddening Abstraction,

You, the Triangulator, the Great Confusor, take note—
for centuries this populace huddled in the earth-walled halls,

smeared black butter on dried fish, spun wool in the dark,
washed their hair in urine and fermented their meat in whey.

How could you ever conquer a land that didn't know bread?
You have left me here to wander, far from friends,

my family shuffling about their small farm
your absent gaze pressing them toward the grave

the night numbing me to the evident good
I might do or understand or receive.

There is a bruise on my brain that does not heal,
nor does it spread, walled in as it is by pills.

Your name is nowhere to be found
in my future, treeless and tasting of salt.

Here I stand at the estuary
My horse cropping grass, no sounds of men

save the one next to me
as he pares dried mutton with a knife.

Geese conduct their exercises nearby
the tide's green hair recedes, pulled backward

by the blue-skinned moon. The wind lifts,
sun flickers, guillemots trim the horizon with their wings

as your great thumb pushes against my lips
and you click the snaffle past my teeth.

Notes

Several years ago while visiting my family home in Wisconsin, I came across a small book of prayers, written in German and published in 1876 in St. Louis. *Der Kleine Gebets-Schatz. Auszug aus dem zu St. Louis, Mo., erschienenen größeren Evang.-Luth. Gebets-Schatz,* is a small, clothbound book made of a size that could be kept in a pocket or reticule. The book exudes utility: during times of duress, this collection of prayers could be consulted, and herein answers could be found. I was moved by the tone of the prayers, and surprised by their specificity. *The Earth Avails* attempts to bring these prayers into my own particular contemporary contexts by fashioning them into poems.

Other poems in this collection refract and adapt several eighteenth- and nineteenth-century folk-religious documents. *Himmelsbriefen,* or Heaven-letters, were common among the Pennsylvania Germans, and were believed to have mystical properties—much like chain letters. Here too, I was drawn to the ways the *Himmelsbriefen* aimed to ward off misfortune and how they showed an abiding wish for language to bind up the world and shield the reader from harm.

The authors of the original documents are anonymous.

The epigraph from "The Anglo-Saxon Bee Charm" is adapted slightly from "For a Swarm of Bees" which appears in *The Anglo-Saxon World: An Anthology from Oxford World's Classics,* Oxford University Press, 1982, and which was translated by Kevin Crossley-Holland.

"Heaven-Letter" was adapted from the Johann Heinrich Dechert of Basel house blessing, Roughwood Collection, Library Company of Philadelphia.

"Dwell in My House" was adapted from the Heinrich Weiss manuscript, 1791 house blessing, Schwenkfelder Library, Pennsburg, Pennsylvania.

The second "Heaven-Letter" is adapted from the Magdeburg Heaven-letter of 1783, Roughwood Collection, Library Company of Philadelphia.

"Fire-Letter" is based on the Kutztown Fire-letter, Roughwood Collection, Library Company of Philadelphia.

Acknowledgments

Grateful acknowledgment is made to the editors of the following publications in which some of these poems have appeared, sometimes in earlier forms and under different titles:

The Academy of American Poets Poem-a-Day, The Awl, Columbia: A Journal of Literature and Art, Devils Lake, Guernica, The Literary Review, Michigan Quarterly Review, Missouri Review, The New Republic, Oxford Poetry (England), *Plume, Poetry, Southern California Review, Tin House,* and *The The Poetry.* "Coyote, with Mange" also appeared in the *2010 Best American Poetry* (Scribner, 2010), in *Being Human* (Bloodaxe Books, 2012), and in *Collective Brightness* (Sibling Rivalry Press, 2011).

A number of these poems also appeared in a limited edition chapbook published by Anomalous Press.

Thank you to everyone at Graywolf Press, especially Jeff Shotts whose guidance helped make this a better book. Also, I am grateful to my colleagues at Bennington College for their many kindnesses and for their inspiring intelligence. A sabbatical leave and grants from the college supported travel and time during which many of these poems were written.

Mary Jo Bang, April Bernard, Carmen Gimenez-Smith, Sarah Messer, Katharine Whitcomb, and Monica Youn offered comments and advice on these poems. I am very grateful to all of you.

Thanks to the boards and staff of Arteles Creative Center in Hämeenkyrö, Finland, and Herhúsið in Siglufjörður, Iceland, for winter residencies during which some of this work was completed.

To James Cancienne, *merci.*

MARK WUNDERLICH is the author of *The Anchorage,* which received the Lambda Literary Award, and *Voluntary Servitude.* He is the recipient of fellowships from the National Endowment for the Arts and the Massachusetts Cultural Council, and his work has appeared in journals such as the *New Republic, Poetry, Tin House,* and the *Yale Review,* and in the *2010 Best American Poetry.* He teaches literature and writing at Bennington College in Vermont and is a member of the core faculty of the Bennington Writing Seminars. He lives in New York's Hudson Valley. More information about the author and his work can be found at: www.markwunderlich.com.

The Earth Avails has been set in Adobe Garamond,
a typeface drawn by Robert Slimbach and based on
type cut by Claude Garamond in the sixteenth century.

Book design and composition by BookMobile Design & Digital Publisher Services,
Minneapolis, Minnesota. Manufactured by Versa Press on acid-free,
30 percent postconsumer wastepaper.